SMcWICK

PALMETTO
PUBLISHING
Charleston, SC
www.PalmettoPublishing.com

Copyright © 2024 by Rose Wamburu

All rights reserved

No portion of this book may be reproduced, stored in a retrieval system, or transmitted in any form by any means–electronic, mechanical, photocopy, recording, or other–except for brief quotations in printed reviews, without prior permission of the author.

Paperback ISBN: 9798822961173

SMOLDERING WICK

Rose Wamburu

Table of Contents

When I Finally Meet You 1
When the Right Time Comes 2
If It Was Tears that Moved God 3
Hope 4
If the Lord Has No Answer. 5
Awaited Dreams 6
This Life 7
The Line Between You and Your Breakthrough . . . 8
When You Miss an Opportunity. 9
Broken Heart 10
Hold on to Your Dreams 11
A Prayer. 13
When They Ask about Love & Marriage 14
Forsaken 15
I Am the CEO of My Destiny. 16
Now that I Am Here. 17
It is Not Easy Being in the Pit 18
May I Never Lose God's Grip 19
Being Single 20
A Prayer. 21
Value 22
How Can One Be Holy? 23
Sometimes, Life Feels Like a Caged Bird 24
May I Never Forget 26
The Things I stopped. 27
It is in Vain to Serve Men 28
How God sees Us 29

The Thing about God.	31
The Irony of Life	32
In a World Full of Hurt	34
God has Appointed You	35
In Life	36
Our Dreams Are Valid	38
Violence in the City	40
Life's Situation	42
I Am Safe with God	44
God's Testimony	45
Our Lord Is Our Sure Foundation	46
Man is Limited	47
God's Got the World in His Hands	48
Do not Live a Life of a Spectator	49
You Tell Me You Have a Plan for Me	50
God's Assurance in Times of Pressure	52
This Year	53
A Prayer	54
Why I Am Crying	55
The Glass Ceiling	56
A Man for Me	57
Marriage Partner	58
Just As I Am	59
Late Bloomer	60
Doubt	62
The One Who Watches Over Me	63
The Road to Success	64
Sometimes Faith	65
I Will Never Give Up	67

Life without Christ	68
Sometimes Life	69
In the Quiet Hours of the Night	71
A Soldier	72
Lord	73
Where I Belong	74
I Am Stepping into This Solid Ground	75
The Life I Want for Me	76
When I Look at You	78
Do Not Call Me Mara	79
Peace	80
No One Knows the Price of War	81
The Voices	83
Somedays	84
The Masks People Wear	85
The Past	86
Not Giving Up on My Dream	87
Hard Questions	88
When He is Not the Right One	89
Beyond This Defeat	90
Life is So Short	91
Miscarried Dream	92
What Is Impossible	94
I Made Peace	95
No Quitting Till It's Done	96
About the Author	97

When I Finally Meet You

The day will come when I meet you
My heart racing
Tears rolling down freely on my face, staining my cheeks
My lips smacking, my nose dripping
I cannot contain myself
I cannot hold myself together
Seeing your face
You who died for me
Putting a face to your name
What a day
When the curtain is finally unveiled
And the light will shine
Mine eyes shall see you,
The one that I have been waiting for

When the Right Time Comes

When the right time comes
The right time is right
Everything comes together
Everything falls in place
When the right time comes
Yes, it's true that there is a right time
And when it comes you know it
You know it because it's like when the day breaks
The light shines, the darkness dissipates
The right time is as clear as fall approaches
Plants change color
Trees shed their leaves, and temperatures fall
The sun shines, but the warmth is different
Yes, when the right time comes, you know
When the right time comes
There is clarity
No darkness
No confusion
You can't make mistakes
things become clear
Just be patient
Your right time is coming

If It Was Tears that Moved God

If it was tears that moved
the heart of God
He could have moved for me a long time
But tears don't move God
I have cried many times
I shed tons and tons of tears
But I find myself crying another day
For the same thing that I cried for yesterday and
the day before
I am still searching
What moves the heart of God?

Hope

Hope hope
Black people hope
White people hope
Have hope
Give hope
Sow hope
Reap hope
Hope hope
Sow hope wherever you can
We need hope
Hold on to hope
Never lose hope

If the Lord Has No Answer

If the Lord does not listen to your cry, who will?
If the Lord has no answer, who does?
If the Lord does not answer you, who will?
Lord, if you do not hear us, who will?
If you do not take away our reproach, who will?
Answer us, Lord,
From your holy hill, do not be silent
Do not ignore our cry
Do not let the enemy mock us

Awaited Dreams

I wish this were a dream
That I would wake up from and realize it is not real
When you wait for something for so long
When you longed for it all your life
Then the day and the thing you have been waiting for comes
It is not like you had envisioned it
The desire is gone
The longing is gone
 The day comes, and now it is passed
I thought that I would be happy forever
I thought I would never forget that day
But the joy was just short-lived
It was a brief bliss
I even no longer have any memories left
I erased all the memories
What was all that longing for?
What was all that waiting for
Now I look around
Sit in silence
In the darkness
All by myself
Thinking about the day, the thing that I waited for

This Life

Life is a contrast
One awakes, another dies in their sleep
One is born, dies a few minutes later
one dies in their youth , others live until they despise life
One is celebrating
Another is moaning
One is getting married while another is getting divorce
One is fruitful, another is barren
One is rich, another is poor
Such is life
It is so and cannot be otherwise
While life is a cycle of contrast
It does not mean we have to stay in one cycle
The wheel of life is always moving and turning
If today you are in the unfavorable part of the wheel
Keep focus, the wheel will eventually turn
And you can fall in the favorable side of the wheel

The Line Between You and Your Breakthrough

The line between you and success
it is paper thin like the edge of a paper
Or like the hair strand
It is also as great and deep like the chasm
that separated Abraham and the rich man
You see it this close
Yet so far
You hold it in your hand but then very slippery
It is elusive
You see it coming so close to it but so far
One small mistake you lose it
When it comes to your breakthrough
You must be at the right place at the right time
You must be razor focused
It is possible for breakthrough to come and miss it
Sometimes breakthrough is camouflaged
It is easy to confuse it
You must be there at the right time
You must pay attention
Your breakthrough is coming
Be ready for it when it comes

When You Miss an Opportunity

It is a serious mistake
When we miss an opportunity
Missed moment
When we focus on the wrong things
We miss the little and important things
In life, focus, pay attention
An opportunity you have waited for long
It can come quickly, like the blinking of an eye
You blink, you lose it
Pay attention
Be alert
Some opportunities are of a lifetime
You miss them, and you live a lifetime of regret
If they come back, it is just a little too late

Broken Heart

No one knows the pain of a broken heart
No one understand the pain of a broken heart
No one knows the cure for a broken heart
There is no medicine for a broken heart.
There is no doctor that can treat a broken heart.
No surgeon can operate on a broken heart
No one can understand a broken heart
Nothing can take away the pain of a broken heart
No amount of words can soothe a broken heart
Nothing can erase or scrub away the pain of broken heart
But there is one who is able
He has the power to heal
He understands how to fix a broken heart
He treats and nurses broken hearts
He is the great physician
If He does not heal your broken heart
You just learn to manage a broken heart
You cease to live, and you are just surviving
Do not live with a broken heart
You suffer for the rest of your life
Ask God to heal your heart
For he is able

Hold on to Your Dreams

How fleetingly life flatters us—
One moment, making plans
One minute you can see, you can feel the future
With your inner eyes
Your dreams and your plans are so close
In your mind, you can even smell them
You can touch them
You are optimistic about life
You are full of Hope
That future holds remarkable things
In your mind you envision the future like the Northern star
That guides you in the night
You are so hopeful you believe you can fly
The next minute, life happens
All the optimism disappears
That bright future you dreamed of starts to disappear
You were a dreamer
You cannot dream anymore
It is like someone clipped your wings
It is like when the clouds cover the sun
You cannot dream
Where did that hope, and optimism go?
Your mind is foggy
In the past, it was clear. You knew what you wanted

Only that lately, you are not sure
No matter how dark life is
Do not give up
Just like that cloud covers the sun
The covering does not stop the sun from shining
Eventually the cloud moves, and we get to see the sun
Hang on to the hope of the glorious future
No matter how gloomy life is
Do not allow yourself to lose the hope
There is still hope for a great tomorrow
Only if you do not give up

A Prayer

Lord, you are Alpha and Omega
The Ancient of Days
The one who founded the earth
The one who spreads the heavens
The one that saves with His mighty hand.
Your eyes see the end from the beginning.
You see when I rise and even when I fall asleep
You know the very number of my days
You have scribbled them in your book
You know my unformed substance,
I am continually in your mind
In the presence of your congregation, I praise you
In the presence of your people, I will praise you
I put my trust in you
I commit my life to you
As you were with Israel, your servant,
Be with me
Guide me
Let your hand be upon me
Let me not be defeated
Let me not be put to shame
When I come to the crossroads of life
When I do not know which way to turn
Show me the way
I look up to you
You will guide me
You will not lead me astray

When They Ask about Love & Marriage

For some people
Love and marriage
It is like north and south
They will never meet
Incompatible, they cannot mix
It is like spilled milk
You try, but you cannot put it back in a bottle
It is like shattered glass
It cannot be pieced together
It is like picking up a snowflake.
It quickly melts
It is like vapor rising in the air Visible yet impossible to hold
Like leaves swept by the wind, they slip right through your fingers.
It is like counting drops of water,
or chasing shadows in the dark a futile endeavor
Like trying to hold fog always elusive forever out of reach
Oh what a chore love and marriage can be
for some
a daunting task, relentless pursuit

Forsaken

Sometimes we are forsaken
But no matter who leaves you
Never forsake yourself
Believe in who you are
There is no other you
No one can believe in you more than you can
There is no better version of you
Always know you are more than enough
You are and have what it takes
By yourself,
With God by your side
You can conquer the world

I Am the CEO of My Destiny

I am the CEO of my destiny, The CFO of my dreams,
The author of my journey, And the artist of my life.

I am the speaker, the director, The conductor of my symphony, The driver of my path,
The pilot of my skies.

I hold the power
To succeed or to stumble, To rise or to fall,
To steer my life in any direction I choose.

I am the author of my story

I direct my life with purpose, Guiding it toward paths of joy and fulfillment.
I paint my life in vibrant hues, Creating the masterpiece I want it to be.

Now that I Am Here

Now that I am here Now what?
You flunked your exam.
You defaulted on a mortgage. You're going through a divorce. You're a single mom.
You lost your job.
You maxed out your credit card. Your relationship fell apart.

Now what, you ask? What do I do?

Sometimes, life throws curveballs, And you're left unsure,
Lost in a sea of doubt,
Wondering if giving up is the only way out.

But while life can be hard, Worrying won't change a thing. Instead, be proactive.
You cannot rewrite the past,
But you hold the pen for your future.

Instead of despair, take a step. Instead of sorrow, rise again.
You may not control what life throws at you,
But you can choose how to respond.

Face the storm, One step at a time,

It is Not Easy Being in the Pit

It is not easy being in the pit
It is complex trying to find your way out
It is hard to see when in the pit
It is hard to think when you are in the pit
Just like David waited patiently on the Lord,
You also may need to wait patiently
He will incline his ears to you
He will hear your cry
It is not easy
But you will get through it
For there is no temptation that is beyond us
And even when we are being tempted
God provides a way out

May I Never Lose God's Grip

May I never lose faith in God
May I never lose the fire
May I never lose hope in God
May I never lose my focus on God
May I never lose sight of God
May I never lose my heart for God
May my love for God never fade
May my love for God grow
May my love for God be deep
May I always be in tune with God.
May I always be one with God

Being Single

Being single and advanced in age
Is not a weakness
It is not a disability
It does not mean you are broken
It does not mean you need fixing
It is not a project that has a deadline
It is not a puzzle that needs to be solved
It is not a problem that needs to be sorted out
You are not lacking
You are not incomplete
You are not empty
It is not a reason to be gloomy
It is not a reason to be sad.
It is not a reason to pity yourself
Being single and advanced in age
It is just a season.
Just like every season has a beginning and an end
Even though your season prolonged it will soon end

A Prayer

My plea to God
Do not allow me to die like a mere man
Do not allow me to die without accomplishing my purpose
Give me a long life to accomplish my purpose
Give me good health that I can accomplish my purpose
Let me know you so that I may know your will for me
Let me leave a mark that I was there
May I be of service to you and your people
Cause me to be a blessing to many
May you never regret creating me
May I live to bring glory to your name
Give me strength and stability
Remove any hindrances
I pray for a defining moment
Help me to reign
Help me to sit in the high places
May my place not be taken by another
May I never miss my blessings
May I know your will for me

Value

We understand the value of money
World currencies are pegged to stronger currencies
Because they need stability
When it comes to God
He does not derive value from another god.
He does not need another power to stabilize Him.
He is all-powerful.
There will never come a time when God is dethroned
Or God has lost value.
God never changes
Everything else changes
Trust in God
Put your hope in Him alone

How Can One Be Holy?

How can one attain your standard of holiness?
While our hearts are impure
Our hands are unclean
We have worshiped idols
We have told lies
We strive to be holy
We strive to lead a holy life
But we are weak
We fall short of your glory
We are constantly on our knees
Yesterday, today, tomorrow, and the day after
We will be on our knees
Praying for your mercies that are new each morning
We try and fail
Because of our shortcomings
We fail many times
We can only rely on your mercies
Only those who have pure hearts can ascend your hill
Those whose hands are clean
 Those who have not worshiped idols
Those whose lips have not spoken lies
I am unclean
I am dependent on your mercies
I am dependent on your unending love
To purify my heart
To cleanse my hands
To help my lips speak the truth

Sometimes, Life Feels Like a Caged Bird

Sometimes, life feels like a caged bird
You are Confused and scared
Like a bird you fluff your feathers to see if you
can escape
You peck the cage to see if you can break free
But the beak is not strong enough to break the cage
Sometimes, life feels like an animal caught in
the thicket
Scared and trying to break free
You wiggle restlessly
In hopes the space can expand and you can break free
An animal trapped in the thicket is scared
Looks all over its surroundings to break free
Or for someone to rescue it
When life feels like you are caged
Or an animal in the thicket
When circumstances are beyond us
The Lord is our deliverer
The Lord is our help
He will deliver us from all our troubles
A beak is not strong enough to break the cage of
an enemy
Neither does an animal have the strength to rescue
itself from the thicket

But the arms of the Lord are strong enough
If you are caged or caught in a thicket
In such a moment of despair
Trust in the Lord
Even though you are caged
There is hope
Hope in the one who can break the cage
Put your hope in one who can break you free from the cage
And you will be able to escape

May I Never Forget

Lord, may I never forget
That it was you who was with me in the forest.
It is you who gave me the strength to kill the bear
That you did not allow the bear to kill me.
You gave me the strength to kill the lion
You did not allow the lion to kill me.
May I never forget you the day I will be a king
May I desire you as I did when I was in the forest
May I never forget you were with me in the caravan
to Egypt
May I never forget that you were with me at
Potiphar's house
May I never forget that you were with me at
Pharaoh's prison
May I never forget you were with me in the fiery furnace
May I never forget that it is you who was with me in the
den of lion
when I become the prime minister
May I always remember that it was you that was with me
May I desire you more than I did when I was in prison

The Things I stopped

I stopped judging others.
I stopped blaming others.
I stopped accusing others.
I stopped judging those who fight
I learned that
You can never understand the pain of judgment until you have been judged
You can never understand the pain until you have been blamed
You will never understand the pain until you are wrongly accused
Until you have something to fight for
You can never understand those who fight
 I have learned to stop talking about others
You will never understand the pain until someone talks about you

It is in Vain to Serve Men

It is great and more rewarding serving God
than serve men
Men are stubborn
They are difficult. Men forget
Men repay good with evil
Men will betray you
Men will break your trust
Ask David after defeating Amalekites; he knows betrayal
Ask Moses in the wilderness and he will tell you about stubbornness
Ask Jesus; they called him Messiah; later they said crucify him
Ask Mordecai after saving the king he was forgotten
Ask Samson when his wife was given to his companion
People forget your works
God never forgets, neither does he lose His records
God's reward is eternal and everlasting.
God is not limited nor bound by time
 Choose God
Look up to Him rather than look up to men.
Desire the glory of God, not the glory of men
The glory of God never fades
The glory of men is fleeting
The glory of men dies and is forgotten
But the glory of God lives forever

How God sees Us

Sometimes, people judge us.
According to our current circumstances.
They define our whole life with one mistake we did
They name us according to our shortcomings
They forget that things change
They call you a failure
Because you have no achievement
You have no status
No accolades to show
They punish you for one mistake you made
They sentence you for life
They mistake your final destiny
With the current place or status, you are in.
They write you off and forget you
But God has not forgotten you
They looked down on David
They saw him as a mere shepherd
They dismissed him as a shepherd boy,
They called him an illegitimate son.
They could not see the king in him
He did not let his role as a shepherd define him
Even being illegitimate did not define him
He did not allow his brothers insults to define him
He was a king
The greatest king in Israel

The man after God's heart
That could be your story
People may have looked down on you
People may have written you out
But that is their story
Their story does not have to be your story
You may have been rejected
You may have been mocked
People may have said hurtful words
Do not let their words get to you
In you, there is greatness
In you there is immense potential.
Just because people do not see what you carry
Do not be blind to what you carry
David's brothers failed to recognize him.
They allowed their prejudice to blind them.
Your family, friends, could be blind with prejudice.
They fail to see
God knows what you carry.
God will announce you.
God will introduce you.
Nothing can hinder God from introducing you.
To their shame, they will see you crowned.

The Thing about God

The thing about God is
He comes at the right time, but not your time.
You cannot put him in a box.
He shows up in unexpected ways
Not how you expect Him.
He answers your prayers in his own ways
Not in your own way
He is a good God regardless
He raises people from poor to rich
He raises people's standards
Like David, he can locate you in life's forest
And place you in a palace
He is a God who gives name to those who are nameless

The Irony of Life

Sometimes, life is as an irony
It is as if life is making a mockery of us
A single woman in the front-row seat of her church
With her hands high, almost touching the roof
Tears rolling down her cheeks, could fill a swimming pool
Praying to God
"Lord help me locate my Boaz," she prays
Behind her, another young woman
engaged a few months ago
Was high in love
But today, she is crying uncontrollably
Her fianc broke off the engagement
To console her, a friend says
"Better a broken relationship than a broken marriage"
Not the words she would want to hear at this time
Her heart is broken and wounded
Many good memories unwilling to let go
But it is over
She must move on
Her neighbor is married, a mother of two
Tired of her marriage and at the edge
She is nauseated at the sight of her husband
She looks for any silly reason for her to exit her marriage

A trigger or opportunity is all she is looking for
So that she can tell her husband "I don't love you anymore"
Another woman a few blocks down
Happily married for ten years but without a child
They have been to many fertilities' clinics
Even explored clinics outside country
Hopeful for breakthrough they can conceive
It is hard to share their story
After many trials and errors, they decide to adopt
A few blocks down, another couple
From the outside, they seem happy
All is going well
Until one morning
Her husband announces, "I want a divorce"
Caught off guard. "What did I do?" she asks.
"It's not you honey" husband answers
"Can we go for therapy?" Wife asks.
"You have done nothing wrong." says the husband.
"It is just that things have changed
We drifted apart," he says.
A few months down the line, divorce is finalized.
The man is marrying another woman
The love of his life, or so he claims.
Life has no balance
Find your own balance

In a World Full of Hurt

In a hurtful world
Choose to sow kindness
In a world filled with hate
Choose to sow love
In a world filled with rejection
Choose to embrace
In a world filled with prejudice,
choose to sow seeds of inclusivity
In a dejected world
Sow seeds of happiness

God has Appointed You

We spend a lot of time waiting for appointments
Forgetting that God has long appointed us.
God has long called us.
Stop waiting on the side
Stop knocking on doors that are not opening
Instead, know that God has appointed you
Start walking in your mandate
If you do not start walking in your mandate
You might die waiting for an appointment that will never come
God has called you and appointed you.
Thats all you need.

In Life

In life, be buoyant
Many things will try to drown you
But you must stay afloat
Be elastic
Many things will test and stretch you
Do not let them break you
Have nine lives like that of a cat
Many things are competing to take you out
Be determined to live
Have the ability to come back like you never left
Many things are competing to get your space
Be determined to stay
Have the ability to recover after setbacks
You will face many setbacks
Be determined to recover and rise up
Have the ability to have no shame
You will face shame but be shameless
Have the ability to absorb shocks
Many things in life will send shockwaves
Be able to absorb the shock
Have a magnetic heart
Attract good things, repel negative things
People will say hurtful things
Be deaf to negativity
Have the ability to forgive and forget

People will hurt you, do not bear the burden
of unforgiveness
Have amnesia for things that hurt you
In life be like a comeback story
Always come back better, greater than before.

Our Dreams Are Valid

Knowing that even in the darkest moments,
You are stronger than you think.

Becoming the one percent, The cream of society.

But years pass,
And the dreams remain unfulfilled. We find
ourselves at the bottom, Struggling to climb up,
Lost, stranded, frustrated.

We realize it's harder than we imagined.
The path is unclear,
The way forward daunting. Yet, we keep trying.

We cannot give up.
The dream of a great life still burns. So we
work harder,
We push further,
Chasing the life we've envisioned.

Never stop dreaming. Never stop chasing.
Do not exchange your dreams for scraps.
If you desire the top, strive for the top. Do not settle
for less.

The bottom is cold and dark, A life of never enough,
Of scraping by in the shadows. But at the top—
The sun always shines brighter. The first beams of
light greet you.

Desire the top. Go for the top. Stop hesitating,
Start reaching.
You cannot afford to give up
Until you stand where the sun always shines.

Violence in the City

It seems like this is the way life is cut out for us
Always on the run
Always looking behind; who is following us?
Always on the wrong side of the law
We have accepted drugs and violence as the acceptable way of life
Who bewitched us?
Who said this is an acceptable way of life?
This is not the way to live
Do we have to live this way?
Why have we accepted and embraced this way of life?
Why don't we question this way of life?
Is this the way things are supposed to be?
Why do we normalize violence and death?
Why have we accepted bloodshed as if it is, okay?
Why have we accepted and diminished the value of life?
Why have we accepted that this is part of our culture
What culture is this?
Young children dying unwarranted death
Paying for the price that no one that no one understand the cost of
When did we say it is okay
For one to die at seventeen?
I refuse this culture.
I refuse to accept this way of life as my own

I want to question this culture
I want to call into question this way of life.
I refuse to join hands and accept that this is the only way to live
Instead, I choose to break the chain
I refuse to feed this cycle
Hoping that without me, the cycle dies
Hoping if I take a stand, this breaks the chain.
Let us all take a stand against drugs and violence.

Life's Situation

The situations we go through in life may differ
But the common denominator is it is tough
You may be prisoner trying to figure out the next step in life after prison
You may be an evicted, single mother
Trying to figure out where to find shelter for your kids
Your marriage may have ended
You are trying to figure out your next step after divorce
It could be your loved one got a terrifying diagnosis
It could be you are in debt and trying to play catch-up
Your loved one passed away,
And you are trying to figure out how to move on without them
Our situations may differ
Our situations are tough and painful
But one thing we have is to fight through
The urge to give up may be strong
And even enticing
But do not give up
It may hurt, it may be tough and rough
But do not give up
We must keep fighting
Sometimes, during our fighting
We may think it is for our own
But just to realize later that it is not our fight

It is a fight for a family, our society, our community,
a generation
Do not give up.
It may be a cause greater than us
Keep fighting.
Do not give up

I Am Safe with God

I am safe with God
My life is much better with God
Because God is reliable
Everyone else is either unreliable or a liar
The government says inflation is transitory
A few months later, we are in a recession
Spouse, my love for you is unconditional
Ten years later, I want a divorce
God's love is unconditional
God's love is steadfast
God's love unwavering
Many things in life will change, but God will not
I am better with God
He is my only true constant in life
He is my best bet

God's Testimony

God's testimony about you
Is more powerful than the testimony of a thousand men
God's testimony is greater than that of men.
A man's testimony is skewed
A man's testimony is flawed
A man's testimony is biased
May be based on their current emotion
Their current state of mind
Man's testimony changes
But God's testimony of you never changes
It is constant
It is better to work hard to please God than to please men.
Men are forgetful. God is not
Men reward you according to the level of their capacity
God's capacity is indefinite
Work hard to please God, not men

Our Lord Is Our Sure Foundation

God is the only sure thing
He is the only immovable thing in this life
Everything else you cannot count on it
You cannot depend on or rely on it
You cannot place a guarantee
Investments lose value
Stock market fails
Economy collapses
Money depreciates
But God does not lose value
God will not collapse,
God will not depreciate
He remains the same
Has never lost value
Never lost His glory nor His splendor
God is perfect
He is God all by himself
Nations rise, nations fall
Kings rise, kings fall
Yet God's kingdom remains
Our God remains the same
He has never changed, and he will never change

Man is Limited

A human being is limited
He is mortal
Times, seasons are beyond his control
A man cannot change what God has ordered
A man cannot change the way day follows the night
Man cannot add an extra second to his life
Times is beyond his control
Man's power and ability is limited
Man cannot change what God has ordered
Like the course of how night follows the day
He cannot change the path of sunlight
He cannot alter the direction of a raindrop
Even with all invention, with all technology
A man cannot replace God
Technology with all its advancement will never replace God
With God, there is nothing that can limit Him
He is a steady and reliable

God's Got the World in His Hands

The Lord holds the world in his Hands
He holds the pillars that hold the earth together
God holds the universe together
God cannot be moved,
God is the sure and firm foundation
He founded the earth
He founded the seas
He founded the four winds
You can put you trust in Him
No one can question the wisdom of God
No one can fully comprehend God's wisdom
How did He stretch the earth?
How did he form the seas?
You can rely on God
His words are true.
You can rely on it

Do not Live a Life of a Spectator

Do not ascribe to a life of a spectator
 Watching others from the sideline
A spectator lives to clap for others
A spectator lives to watch others
Do not always watch others
Let others watch you, too
Do not live to sing for others
May they also sing for you
Do not live on the sideline
Be the center

You Tell Me You Have a Plan for Me

I look up to you
For you are my rest and my stay
I wait for you, rocking my heart back and forth
Just like a mother rock her baby to sleep
But this is not a mother rocking her baby
It is me waiting eagerly for your promises
The promises you made to me
I look on the horizon to see if anything approach
I search in my spirit
I can barely see
My spiritual eyes fail me.
They are foggy
They are crowded with tears
Sometimes I wonder if I made a wrong turn
Sometimes I think I did not hear you correctly
I do not even know when I made a wrong turn
Sometimes I wonder if I should go back?
Should I start again?
You told me to wait.
I waited
You told me to be patient.
I was patient
You told me to watch and pray.
I did
But even now, I am still waiting,

I am searching in my soul
What could I have done differently?
But I have no answer
Why do I keep missing out?
Is it that I do not look too hard?
Is it that I do not fight hard on my knees?
Is it that I do not fight long enough on my knees? I do not know
If there was anything different to do, I could have done it.
My heart is worn out from waiting
That there is nothing that I can do; I just must wait
The wait is long
The wait is tedious
Hopefully, this time
I have waited long enough
Hopefully, this time the promise is fulfilled

God's Assurance in Times of Pressure

Sometimes, life feels heavy with pressure,
Like a container on the verge of bursting.
One more force, one more strain, And everything spills over.

Our minds, too, overflow— Ready to explode with worries. To-do lists piling high,
Missed deadlines, Missed goals,
Opportunities slipping away. Everything demands our attention, Yet time seems so scarce.

When your mind becomes a battlefield, A war raging in every corner,
Chaos closing in—
Then comes a gentle, reassuring voice:

"I make wars cease to the ends of the earth.
I break the bow,
Cut the spear in two,
Burn the chariot in the fire.
Be still and know that I am God."

What an assurance,
What peace in the midst of the storm.

This Year

This year, do not hope to open a business
Do not hope to go to college
Do not hope to travel
Do not hope that your relationship will get better
Do not hope that your man will propose
Do not hope you will get organized
Do not hope you will pray a lot
Or hope to attend church more
This year, plan to do it and do it
This year, be a doer
This year, let go of what has not worked in the past
The highest probability is
If something has not worked in the past
It will not start working right now
Life is about patterns
Look at your past
Look at your trail
What does it tell you?
Follow the pattern or break the pattern

A Prayer

Do not allow me to live like a fool
Do not let me die the death of a fool
Foolish men live like there is no tomorrow
They lead life as if it is their own, forgetting
God has lent life to them
Someday God will require an account of how
we lived
May I die empty
Give me strength and stability
Remove anything that hinders me
I do not want to live a life without a purpose
May I not be that walking prince
May I not be a fool in high position
Set me in my rightful position in life

Why I Am Crying

He saw me shed tears in the church
Later, he saw me smile
He was confused

He asked if I was okay. "I saw you
crying earlier."

I replied, "Yes, everything is okay.
I replied, "It is life.
We all go through rough days"

Emotional about losses, unattained goals,
pressure at work, pressure at home
I was just crying my heart out

In a few minutes, I felt relieved
Sometimes, we are under pressure
Whatever gives you relief.
If it is good, do it.

The Glass Ceiling

I am getting ready to crack open the glass ceiling
But I do not know how
I do not know what tools to use
My toolbox is empty
I wonder what tools I need?
Someone suggested
Try prayers
Try meditation
Try working hard
Try excellence
Breaking glass ceiling is not easy
It is not a straight shot
It requires trying different tools
It requires being consistent
Sometimes it takes knowing a person
Sometimes it means hitting hard
Hitting one point many times
Until you break resistance
Until you create a weak point; I am trying
I keep trying the only way I know how
I must break the glass ceiling of my life
I keep trying harder and harder
Someone tell me
What is the secret to cracking the glass ceiling?
One thing, though, is do not give up
One day it will crack open

A Man for Me

There are so many men in this world
If the Lord willed to give me one
He could pluck one from any corner of the earth
From North, South, East, or West
But he has not done that
Some men are tall while others are short
Some are wide, others are narrow
I just want the one who will love me
The one who will draw me close to God
The chief priest of our home
That is the one I have been waiting for
And not the one who will draw me away from God
The one with whom I will grow old together
The one with whom I will serve the Lord together.
That is the man for me.

Marriage Partner

Finding the marriage partner
Finding the right husband or wife
Is like looking for a needle in a haystack
Or searching for a pebble on the river bend
It is like searching for one grain of sand in an ocean
Or just choosing one fish in a school of fish
You know he is there, but not found just anywhere
You know he is among the grains of sand, but not just any grain
You know he is among the school of fish, but not just any fish
You know he is one in the population of many, but not just any
You know he is not just anyone
Oh, what a chore it is to find the right one
The right one is like stoking of fire
Burns steadily, does not lose control
He is not like gasoline
Burns quickly and then goes off
Finding the one person to spend my entire life with
To grow old with
Is a task
 I know there is one out for me.
I know there is one for me

Just As I Am

As I approach your throne
I pray earnestly
Just as I am
Lord, I come to you
In your presence
I bear it all
I know that there is nothing that I can hide from you
There is no sin that you cannot forgive
I know you have not written me out
I am not totaled
I am not beyond redemption
I am not beyond repair
I cannot run away from your presence
I have nowhere to hide
Your presence fills the earth
I cannot run away; I cannot hide
Instead, I will come to you as I am
For you are a merciful God

Late Bloomer

Winter has ended
And spring is beginning
All dead trees are coming alive
A leaf here, a leaf there, they are starting to bud
I remember my flowerpot
At the backyard
I go out to check see
If it is budding
It is just a dead shrub with no signs of life in it
Thought of throwing the flowerpot away
But then I decided to give it a few days
Every day, I go to the backyard
To see if there is a sign of life
I go back disappointed
There is no sign of life
Still do not want to throw away my flower
Every day at the back of my backyard, I look around
All other flowers have bloomed
But my flower is dead, and no sign of life
After days and weeks of no signs of life
I decide to throw the pot and the dead shrub
Just one glance before I dump it
Then, to my surprise there it is
A little green bud
My flower is alive

I will keep it
I will not throw it away
Each day, the bud gets bigger
And then, one day, there is my flower
Beautiful yellow flower
I call it a late bloomer
Just give it time, and it will bloom

Doubt

Sometimes I am vulnerable
Sometimes, I have doubted
Sometimes, I question you
I have come to you wounded
I search for your presence
In those moments I cannot find you
I do not feel your presence, but I know you are there
When I am weak, you reassure me
Many times, you speak to me through the word
You encourage and uplift me
Even when I feel abandoned
I know you have not abandoned me
The truth about the journey of faith is that it is not smooth
It has bumps
It can be rough
Thank you for reassuring me
Hold my hand
Do not let go of me

The One Who Watches Over Me

He who watches over Israel is watching me
He will not forsake me
He will not let my feet stumble,
He will not slumber. He is faithful.
God is gracious
He is faithful, and he will never let go of me.

The Road to Success

Who has been on the road to success?
The road to success is not a straight one
It has many turns and twists
There is neither narrow nor wide path that
leads you to success
It is a web
It is a labyrinth
It is a puzzle
You go up and down, sideways
There is no road map to success
There is no GPS
There are no pointers to success
One does not even know when they get there
Everyone has their own definition of success
To a person born in poverty, money is success
A person who has no shelter
A roof over their head is success
As for me, success is knowing God
Success is knowing His will for me
Success is carrying out His purpose for my life
That is success.

Sometimes Faith

Sometimes, our faith is tried
Our faith is shaken
Our faith is tested
Sometimes, seeds of unbelief are sowed
When we look at the reality of life
Just like Peter,
We want to hear Jesus ask us to come
We want Jesus to stretch over his hand to us
Ask us to walk on the water
When we look at the reality
We become like Peter
At first, we believed that we could walk on water
We even take the first step
Then we doubt and we start to sink
We tell ourselves the realness of the things we are facing
The reality is just too real
The fear is more vivid
We fear more than we have faith
We become like the disciples when they saw Jesus
They thought he must be a ghost
We tell ourselves maybe our faith is just a ghost
We justify our fear with the things we are facing
How can faith be real, we ask
When retirement is just around the corner and there are no savings?

How can we have faith when our house is
in foreclosure?
How can faith be real when you are childless
The reality of life versus our faith
How can we have faith when our child dies of suicide
How can we have faith when someone takes away the
life of our loved one
The reality of life sometimes makes us like Peter
we doubt, we preach to ourselves
We tell ourselves
It is one thing to hear Jesus turned water into wine
It is one thing to read that He fed 5,000 people
It is another thing to have Christ real in your life.
Sometimes, we need a miracle
The reality of life versus our faith
It is our faith-tested
In the end, let your faith triumph over fear
Because even Jesus overcame
We must also overcome

I Will Never Give Up

After all is said and done
I have vowed to myself
I will never give up
Even if the Earth shifts
The sky moves higher. I will never give up
Even in the grave, I will never give up
To give up, I will never
No matter the circumstances
No matter how grim the report is
No matter how dire the situation is
I refuse to give up
No matter how many no's I get
I will keep trying
Even if the door is locked
I will peep through the window or the keyhole
I will knock till my knuckles are sore
I will knock till I wear you out and you open
I will keep showing up till your eyes are sore at seeing me
I will never give up
And that is the fighter spirit in me

Life without Christ

Life without Christ is meaningless
It is a life without direction
It is a life without a purpose
You try many things
Until you come to realization how futile life is without Christ
You give up leading yourself
Doing things your way
And humbly come to the Lord
You go to his cross
And surrender all to him
Life Without Christ is like walking in the darkness
You can only go so far
If you want to go far in life
Go with Christ
Do not walk on your own
Do not rely on your own wisdom
Choose to ask the Lord for direction
Rely on His counsel
Without His counsel
You are busy but doing nothing
What He asks of you, be ready to do
I realize how futile my ways are without God
I want to try His ways

Sometimes Life

Sometimes, life plays tricks on us
Just like your mind tricks you when you are in the dessert
After walking thousands of miles
Thirsty and out of water
You keep seeing a mirage of an oasis
You keep walking towards it
The closer you get, the further it moves
In the beginning it raises your hopes
You continue walking towards it
But it moves further
It keeps moving further from you
So is lifelike a mirage
Like Sarah, in the Bible
When waiting on God's promises
You wait
You know you have waited for long
There is no way you can wait anymore
You do not even have the strength and the time
You have run out of patience
Do not even have any more prayer lines
In your mind
The only prayer line you have
Is one line of giving thanks
But just like the mirage in the desert

You felt your moment of breakthrough was close.
It is right at hand
But instead, it keeps moving away further
Your breakthrough tarries:
You realize there is more waiting,
More wrestling to do
While a mirage is an illusion
It does not exist
The walk is not, the prayer is not
The more you keep at it
The closer you get to real water
Soon your prayers will be answered
You will celebrate

In the Quiet Hours of the Night

In the quiet hours of the night
Sometimes, I meditate on your love
Other times, I toss and turn
Sleep escapes me
And my mind wanders
A loving God
You love me
Yet you deny me the things I desire
You said if a child asks for bread
A father will not give them a stone
Things that I long for with my whole being
Sometimes, I am lost
Why would you claim to love me
Yet, withhold the one thing I desire?
I cannot wrap my mind around love and denial
When will you hear me
When will you answer my prayer?

A Soldier

My heart is wounded
My heart is broken
My pride bruised
I am in pain
I am in anguish
But I am undeterred
I am relentless
Even if you do not answer my prayers today
I will press on
Even though I hurt
Even though my knees are sore
Even though my tears are dry
And my eyes are irritated
I know one day, my prayer will be answered
And it will erase all the pain
I will forget the frustration
I will forget the wait
I know that day is coming

Lord

I hand over to you my broken pieces
I roll over my pain to you
I roll over my tears
I roll every piece to the cross
I refuse to continue carrying burdens
I hand them over to you
Mend my broken heart
Piece my heart together
Heal my heart

Where I Belong

There is peace
Love and joy
No chaos
It is quiet and calm
Where one never lacks
There is plenty
There is no emptiness

I Am Stepping into This Solid Ground

Bold and fearless and without care

Even though I am bold, fearless, and without care

Winds and storms try to bring me down

The sail may be torn, but it will weather the storm

Because the Lord directs me

I know he will guide me safely

I know he will be my anchor

I have gone through many storms

I know how rough the storms can be

I know how it is, being tossed to the bottom of the sea

But I remain strong

I never give up

I just keep looking up to Him for help

The Life I Want for Me

The life I want for me
I refuse to live a handout life
The life of hand to mouth
I refuse a life of overdraft
I refuse to live a paycheck-to-paycheck life
I refuse to dream a regular dream
A nice house, nice car
I want the best things of life
I refuse the common person mentality
I want wonderful things in life
I want to live like the child of a king
Because that is who I am
I refuse to work for stomachs and bills sake
I refuse to work for work's sake
I refuse to hand over poverty to the next generation
I want to make a difference
I want to spearhead
I want to breakthrough
I want to run over and overflow
I want to go where no one else has been
I want to leave a trail
I want to trailblaze
I want to break barriers
I want to go up
I want to live a life of legacy

I want to hand over inheritance to the next generation
I want a hundred years from now
Someone will know I existed
That is the kind of life I want

When I Look at You

I see God's great men and women
I see excellency engraved in you
I see a great future carved in you, sculpted, molded
I see God's greatest vessel of our time
I see God's greatest plan in sketches,
awaiting completion
I see God's greatest purpose
I see God sowing seeds of greatness in you
I see the word of God like water
I see God watering you until you sprout and become
a plant
I see you like a plant that bears fruits
I may not know what kind of fruit
But surely, I see good fruit in you
You are like clay in the potter's hand
God is your potter
He is refining you
Only He who knows the final product
But I know that it is a high-quality product
When I look at you
I see God's great army
An army that cannot be defeated, formidable
An army that has made God its commander
An army that God wins their battle
An army that is always victorious
No matter the battle being waged on them
Gods' army emerges victorious

Do Not Call Me Mara

Do not call me Mara
Because I am no longer bitter
Do not call me barren
I am no longer barren
God has made me fruitful
He has made me a mother to nations
I am no longer single
God has made me a multitude,
God has made me a nation of people
I am no longer broken
God has mended my heart
I am not moaning
God has made me to rejoice
I am no longer forgotten
God has remembered me
From now on call me blessed

Peace

I pray for peace
I pray for peace to prevail
I pray for the peace of God
The peace that surpasses all human understanding
May peace fall like rain
May the peace of God flow like a mighty river
May peace prevail in every city
Peace prevails in every village
Peace prevails in every family
Peace prevails in the nations of the earth
May the peace of God and not the peace that man gives
May that peace prevail

No One Knows the Price of War

No one knows the price of war
No one can afford the price of war
No one understands the fear caused by war
The terror caused by war
Apart from the victim of war
Who goes to bed not knowing what to expect tomorrow
They fall asleep to the noise of shelling
And wakes up to the sounds of bombs being dropped
Marching sounds of the soldier's boots
Who calculates the loss caused by war?
Who can restore the lives lost?
Who can restore bloodshed?
Is there therapy that can heal the trauma caused by war?
Is there a policy that can the price of
destabilizing communities?
Nothing can measure the price, or the loss caused
by war
Only the victim who understands
Who can negotiate for peace?
Do they understand the urgency?
Do they understand the need?
If there is any hope for peace
It does not exist in any of the world's leaders
Peace does not lie in any of the world's organizations
Peace does not lie in any country

Whether great or small, rich, or poor
The hope for world peace lies in Christ
He is the prince of peace
Any other hope is a lie
Peace can only come from God
For He is a God who understands war
And he knows the terms of peace
Men who negotiate for peace have no understanding
They are deaf to the cries of the people
They are blind to the pain and suffering of the people
They negotiate for peace from the lofts of
their skyscrapers
 miles and miles away from the terror
They come to witness the horror of war from their
heavily guarded choppers
As if to mock the victims
How do you understand the suffering from
Washington, DC or from Buckingham palace?
How do you understand the suffering with a day's visit?
How can you understand the urgency?
Only God understands
If there is a true advocate for peace
The true advocate is God

The Voices

The voices that tell me to give up are loud
They deafen my ears
They say I will never make it
Sometimes, it is as if they win
They overwhelm me
They corner my mind and my spirit
They keep me in darkness
But even in those dark moments, I refuse to surrender
I deny them victory
I must drown them
If they are loud, I must be louder
I drown them with worship
I drown them with praise
I must overcome
I must conquer them by the blood
And by the name of Jesus

Somedays

Somedays, I am just surviving
Some days, I just want to forget
I just want to see the day end
With the hope that tomorrow will be a better day
Today, I am not worried about tomorrow
I just want to get through this moment,
To watch today quietly slip away.
I simply want to survive today.
For each day brings its own trouble
I want today's troubles to be gone

The Masks People Wear

There are many masks that people wear—
Some visible, others unseen.

Some masks are for protection, While others are meant to hide.
Behind these masks lie broken hearts, Shattered spirits, Dreams left unfulfilled.

Behind the masks are fake smiles, Disguising pain and disappointment. Behind them are quiet, muted voices, Afraid to speak,
Knowing one word might unleash a flood of tears.

Behind the masks are aching hearts, Hurting in silence.

Some masks are sunglasses, Hiding puffy, tear-streaked eyes. Others take the form of makeup, Concealing scars and wounds

Oh, the many masks that people wear—
Layers upon layers to shield their pain.

Would you like to develop this further or shift the tone?

The Past

The past is past
There is absolutely nothing we can do about it
The best thing we can do about the past
Is to make peace with it
Is to let go of the past
The past may have been beautiful
The past marked with pain
Good memories
Lost opportunities
In the past you could have been successful
In the past you could have been a hero
Let the past be the past
Bury the past in the ocean
Allow yourself to heal from the pain of the past
Forget the success of the past
Allow yourself to see other opportunities
But you must allow the past to be past
If you do not let, go of the past
You will live to be a captive of the past
You remain stuck
You will never know the vast opportunities that await you

Not Giving Up on My Dream

I will not give up on my dream
Even though I have tried many times
Even though each time I have failed
Even though I have failed more times than I can keep count
I will never give up on my dream
I keep trying
My dream does not have to make sense to everyone
It is not meant to impress everyone
I will not give up on my dream
I have knocked on so many doors
Some opened and others were shut
Even then I will not give up
One day the door will open
And that will change everything
I will never give up on my dream
Some people said I am overly ambitious
Others said it is fantasy
Even though the naysayers were more than Yes
I still will hang on to my dream

Hard Questions

Sometimes I have questions I ask
Sometimes they have no answer
Sometimes they remain just thoughts in my head
At times I ask
Why does it feel like the Lord is slow?
Why does it feel as if the Lord is slow to act?
Why does it feel like you take sides?
Do you favor some people over others?
Like you loved Jacob and hated Esau
When I cannot wait a minute longer
I want you to be God
I want you to swoop in
When I cannot wait anymore
I want you to act quickly, and with finality.

When He is Not the Right One

When a man or woman is not in love
They are easily irritated
It does not matter what you do to them
Whatever you do becomes an irritation
No matter how good your intentions are
 No matter how important your act is
It is just an irritant
Even if your heart was removed and given to save their life
A person who doesn't loves you, they will find an issue
A man or a woman who is not in love speaks in parables
You think this is what they want; you give them
They say, "That is not what I asked"
You give them everything, but it is never enough
A man or a woman who is not in love is an irritant
It is not you who is the problem.
It's just that they do not love you

Beyond This Defeat

Beyond the pain you are going through
Beyond the tear that you shed
Beyond the sorrow you are going through
Beyond the devastation that you are going through
Beyond the brokenness that you are going through
Beyond the sadness that you are going through
Beyond the dryness
There is a Great God
His face may be hidden by the things that you are going through
But he will surely shine upon you
He will come to your rescue
He promises that sorrow may last for a night
But His joy comes in the morning
He is faithful, he keeps his promise of love to those who trust in him
He will provide and give rest to the restless
He will give strength to those who are weak
He will give peace to the peaceless
He will make wells of water in the wilderness
Beyond every challenging situation you are going through
There is a God who will deliver you

Life is So Short

I have learned that life is so short.
One moment, you are here,
You are with your friends and family
Laughing, joking playfully taking things for granted
And then, suddenly, they're gone.
For a season you are like lost sheep without a shepherd
How I pray that I would cherish the time I spend with my loved ones
To savor every fleeting moment.
Because we live on borrowed time
No one knows about tomorrow
How I pray not to take anything for granted
I do not know how much time I have
I do not know how long my loved ones have
While I pray that we will all live long
I know it is a mystery to know how much time is left
Spend the time you have well
You never know why you meet the people you meet
Why do good things have to be brief?
I hope we will be together again
I hope and wish it would be soon
I hope time and events of life do not take away my good friends

Miscarried Dream

Sometimes in life we face mishaps
You are expectant
Beautiful moment
Uncontrollable joy
Looking forward to hold a baby
Then the unexpected happens
You miscarry
Life goes by
As if nothing happened
And you also must move on
Even though you hurt
May your mouth be full of praise
May your heart be filled with joy
Even though you miscarried
You know God was in the process of doing
Something new in your life
But even now that you have miscarried
God will still do something new
The Lord who helped you conceive your dream
Will help you conceive again
He will make you a mother of many dreams
Run back to His presence
Though the dream is dead
still praise Him
Remember he is also able to resurrect

Your womb will still carry a generation
 miscarriage is painful
But God's deliverance is sweet
Even though your heart is broken and crushed
Even though there is no song in your heart
God will give you new songs
The Lord will show you beyond death there
is life
Beyond moaning there is rejoicing
In God there is restoration
God will fill your heart with praises
He will let your feet dance
He will surely plant another seed in you
He will give you another dream
God will make the womb of your dream fruitful

What Is Impossible

What is impossible with men
Is possible with you, God
Facing rough patches?
Feel like you have reached the end?
There is no impossibility with God?
Trust the process
It may feel like time is gone
It may feel like you have reached the end
But know one day
You will stand and testify

I Made Peace

Sometimes I must remind myself
That I may not be like Hannah
I may not be like Anna of Phanuel
I may not be like Elizabeth
I may not be like Mary
I may not be Joseph
I must remind myself that sometimes I am like Sarah
When the going gets tough, I tweak things
I may be like Moses; sometimes I get angry
Sometimes I may be like Abraham; I lie
Sometimes I may be like Esau; I want instant gratification
Sometimes I am like King Saul; I am impatient
Sometimes I am like Peter; I doubt
God knows I want to be like Hannah
 Persist on my knees till my prayers are answered
I want to be Joseph, forgive those who betray me
 I want to be like Anna, spend more time praying
While I may not be like Anna, Hannah, or Joseph
I cannot give up trying

No Quitting Till It's Done

When life feels like it has lost its meaning
It's as if life has become darkness with no end
in sight
When life feels like flooding without an end
When life feels like a ranging storm with nowhere
to hide
When life stings and you can't take anymore
We just have to push ourselves
just a little bit more
push yourself one more time
One last time
We cannot and have no room for doubt
The only choice we have is win or win
We have no other choice but to believe in ourselves
We have to remind ourselves that we can't quit
We can't quit yet
Till it's all done
We can't quit till we throw the last shovel
We can't quit yet until we see the very end
No quitting till all work is done
No quitting until we exhaust all possibility
We can't quit because winners are losers who chose
not to quit

About the Author

Rose Wamburu is a first time writer from Indiana. My inspiration is from scripture and life in general.